Introducing
THE GLASGOW BOYS

Glasgow Museums

First published in 2010 by Culture and Sport Glasgow (Museums)

ISBN 978-0-902752-93-1

Authors: Jean Walsh and Hugh Stevenson
Edited by: Kim Teo, with thanks to Roger Billcliffe and Fiona MacLeod
Designed by: Fiona MacDonald
Photography for Culture & Sport Glasgow (Museums): Maureen Kinnear
Picture research: Winnie Tyrrell
Digital imaging: Alan Broadfoot

Printed in Scotland by Allander

Prints of pictures © Culture and Sport Glasgow (Museums) can be ordered from
www.glasgowmuseums.com/photolibrary

www.glasgowmuseums.com

Cover image:
Hard at it, 1883,
by James Guthrie

Acknowledgements

All efforts have been made to trace copyright holders but if any have been inadvertently omitted, please notify the publishers. The publishers gratefully acknowledge the following for permission to reproduce illustrations:

Aberdeen Art Gallery & Museums Collections: p. iv; pp. 32–33*; p. 38
Annan Photographs, image from www.annanphotographs.co.uk: p. 6
Collection Miss Flure Grossart: p. 42, 2nd image
Dundee Art Galleries and Museums, Dundee City Council: pp. 4–5
Fife Council Libraries and Museums: Kirkcaldy Museum & Art Gallery, photograph Antonia Reeve Photography: p. 42, 1st image
© The Fleming-Wyfold Art Foundation: p. 54*
© Hunterian Museum and Art Gallery, University of Glasgow: pp. 18&19; p. 30
Museum of Fine Arts, Ghent © Lukas-Art in Flanders vzw: p. 8, 2nd image
National Gallery of Ireland: p. 17*
National Gallery of Scotland: p. 8, 1st image; p. 9; p. 24; pp. 56&57*; p. 66
Paisley Art Institute Collection, held by Paisley Museum, Renfrewshire Council: p. 51
Paisley Museum, Renfrewshire Council: p. 16
Private Collection, courtesy of Pyms Gallery, London: pp. 12&13*; p. 15*
Private Collection, photographer Peter Schächli, Zürich: p. 47*
Private Collections: pp. 10–11; p. 20; p. 21, 2nd image; pp. 28&29; pp. 34&35; pp. 40&41*; p. 43; p. 48; p. 49; p. 50; p. 60, 1st image; p. 60, 2nd image
Robertson Collection, Orkney: pp. 58&59
Scottish Gallery, Edinburgh, and Ewan Mundy Fine Art, Glasgow: p. 61
Scottish National Portrait Gallery: p. 45
Trustees of the Cecil Higgins Art Gallery, Bedford: p. 55*
Yale Center for British Art: p. 39; p. 64, 1st image

All images marked * and those on p.46 and pp.52 & 53 are by courtesy of Felix Rosenstiel's Widow and Son Ltd, London, on behalf of the Estate of Sir John Lavery

Contents

Introduction

To Pastures New, 1882–3
James Guthrie

Aberdeen Art Gallery &
Museums Collections

In this painting Guthrie
has recorded an everyday
scene, emphasizing the
natural tones and colours
of the outdoors. He
has created a sense of
movement, in a way that
was daring for the time,
by cutting off one of the
geese at the edge of the
canvas.

The Glasgow Boys were the most significant group of artists working in Britain at the end of the nineteenth century. They were admired in Europe and America, where they were regularly invited to exhibit, and achieved recognition and widespread popularity at home.

They were a loose-knit group of about 20 artists, linked by friendships and, for the most part, by connections with Glasgow, where they lived, studied or had studios. In the 1880s the British press began to refer to them as 'The Glasgow School of Painters', but the artists themselves could not agree on a name and just referred to each other as 'The Boys'. There was no formal leader, though James Guthrie and William York Macgregor are often described as the most influential. During the period 1880–1900, when the Glasgow Boys produced their best work, there was a core group that included, in addition to Guthrie and Macgregor, Joseph Crawhall, George Henry, EA Hornel, William Kennedy, John Lavery, James Paterson and EA Walton.

The Glasgow Boys rejected the style of painting that was dominant in Scotland at the beginning of their careers. Both prevailing taste and the most prestigious art institution, the Royal Scottish Academy, Edinburgh, favoured sentimental scenes, historical dramas and Highland landscapes. These were painted in studios, by artists who often mixed their pigments with megilp, a sticky liquid that made their paint shiny and which darkened with age. The Glasgow Boys showed their disdain when they called such painters 'Gluepots'.

Instead, they were inspired by a number of artists working in Holland, France and London, especially Jules Bastien-Lepage and James McNeill Whistler. They began painting in a more matter-of-fact way and often worked out of doors. They also adopted Bastien-Lepage's practice of using flat-ended paintbrushes which left square brushstrokes, a distinctive hallmark of the Glasgow Boys' earlier works. At first they painted rural people and landscapes. Later they depicted the inhabitants of Glasgow's affluent suburbs. Eventually, colour, texture and pattern came to be more important.

Pauvre Fauvette, 1881
Jules Bastien-Lepage
Kelvingrove Art Gallery and Museum, Culture and Sport Glasgow

The Glasgow Boys greatly admired Bastien-Lepage. As
here, he often painted a single figure in a rural landscape
set below a high horizon line – an approach many of the
Boys emulated.

Arrangement in Grey and Black, No. 2: Portrait of Thomas Carlyle, 1872–3
James McNeill Whistler

Kelvingrove Art Gallery and Museum, Culture and Sport Glasgow

Whistler was a hero of the Glasgow Boys, as much for his controversial essays challenging established ideas about art as for his paintings with their restrained colour and carefully balanced compositions.

Interior of a Peasant's Cottage, about 1898
Thomas McEwan

Glasgow Museums Resource Centre, Culture and Sport Glasgow

This is a typical 'Gluepot' painting, as derided by the Glasgow Boys. The overly sentimental content and the generally dark tonality were qualities that they particularly disliked.

In their search for new
subjects, the Glasgow Boys
often painted out of doors
in the countryside, their
preferred terrain being
flat, almost characterless
agricultural land.

A Lincolnshire Pasture, 1882
Joseph Crawhall
The McManus: Dundee's Art Gallery & Museum

Some of the Glasgow Boys at Cockburnspath in 1883.
In the front row from the left: EA Walton, Joseph Crawhall,
James Guthrie and James Whitelaw Hamilton. Behind is
Walton's brother George, a Glasgow Style furniture designer.

Painting in Rural Scotland

In the early 1880s several of the Glasgow Boys were pursuing a realist style of painting. Some – including Henry, Guthrie, Walton, Crawhall, Macgregor and Paterson – spent summers painting in rural Scotland, following the example of Jules Bastien-Lepage, who painted at the small French village of Damvillers. The villages of Brig o'Turk, Crail, Moniaive and in particular Cockburnspath all provided subjects. Whether painting rural labourers working in the fields, cottage gardens of villagers or local children returning home from school, the Glasgow Boys sought to record daily life.

This was a time of experimentation for the Glasgow Boys. They had to overcome artistic challenges that came from painting outside, such as depicting figures in a landscape and capturing the effects of light and shade. They also explored painting in watercolour, a medium that was relatively new to them. They hoped to create works that would sell at exhibitions, in some cases relying on doing so to finance their summer painting expeditions.

During the winter months most of the Boys returned to Glasgow, where the centre of instruction and discussion was Macgregor's studio. But in the winter of 1883–84 Guthrie remained near Cockburnspath, with the aim of getting to know the village better by experiencing it in all seasons. He soon missed the company and encouragement of his fellow artists and even contemplated returning to his former life as a law student. Fortunately, other Glasgow Boys returned the next summer.

Painting out of doors together led to a cross-fertilization of ideas, and spurred them on to produce some of their best works. This included the large-scale exhibition pieces for which they were aiming.

A Hind's Daughter, 1883
James Guthrie
National Gallery of Scotland, Edinburgh

Painted in the sombre light of approaching winter, Guthrie's first major Cockburnspath picture borrows elements from Bastien-Lepage, such as the placing of the girl against a high horizon.

Schoolmates, 1884–5
James Guthrie
Museum of Fine Arts, Ghent

The surface of this painting shows that Guthrie made several changes to get the balance of his composition correct. He took great care over the portrayal of the local children's faces.

The Herd Boy, 1886
Edward Arthur Walton
National Gallery of Scotland, Edinburgh
Purchased with the assistance of the Art Fund, 2007

The scale and powerful impact of *The
Herd Boy* illustrate Walton's aim to paint
large exhibition pictures in watercolour,
which gave the medium an importance
it had never had previously.

By painting the girls against the backdrop of a wall, and excluding sky or other surroundings, Henry concentrates our attention on the children and creates a strong design.

Playmates, 1884
George Henry
Private Collection

Painting in France

Several of the Glasgow Boys trained in Paris. They studied in ateliers, informal studios where young artists came to learn from established painters. There they gained experience in rendering light and shade – tonal values – then the root of all French teaching.

In the early 1880s, a number of them – including Arthur Melville, John Lavery, William Kennedy, Thomas Millie Dow and Alexander Roche – left Paris to visit the artists' colony at Grez-sur-Loing, south-west of Paris on the edge of the Barbizon Forest. Grez was attracting painters, writers and musicians – including Robert Louis Stevenson and Frederick Delius – from many countries in Europe, America and even Japan.

The Boys mixed with like-minded artists and worked in a naturalist style. They painted out of doors, depicting the everyday life of the villagers and were inspired by the tranquil River Loing and the quality of the light. Lavery was particularly receptive to the artistic innovations he saw around him and produced some of his finest paintings.

Although they were in a different location, the Glasgow Boys in France created works that were similar in spirit and style to those painted by their counterparts, such as Guthrie and Walton, in Cockburnspath.

Under the Cherry Tree, 1884
John Lavery
Private Collection

Many Glasgow Boys' paintings from both France and Scotland feature a high horizon line, have an emphasis on foreground detail with an atmospheric background, and feature local people as the principal subjects.

Here two women are shown sewing in the enclosed riverside garden behind the Hôtel Chevillon, where many of the artists stayed.

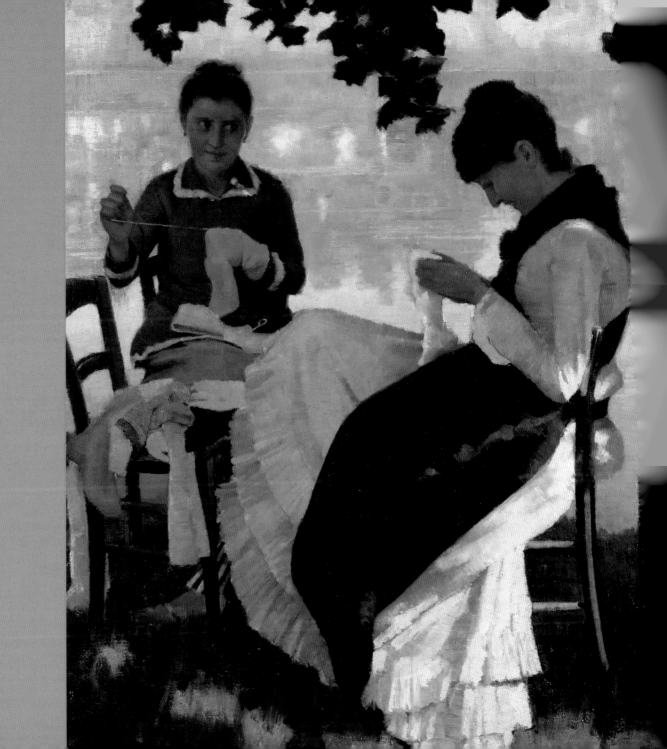

Spring, 1884
William Kennedy
Paisley Museum, Renfrewshire Council

The Glasgow Boys painted many pictures of
children in cottage gardens or orchards. In
this portrayal of happy childhood, Kennedy
uses the blossom, flowers, foliage and trees
to create a lively surface pattern.

On the Bridge at Grez, 1884
John Lavery
National Gallery of Ireland, Dublin

Lavery was one of the few Glasgow Boys who recorded
the daily pursuits of fellow artists. Here he shows his
Irish friend Frank O'Meara with his painting equipment.

The Inspiration of Kirkcudbright and Moniaive

The small town of Kirkcudbright in south-west Scotland was Edward Hornel's hometown. Many of the Glasgow Boys visited, including Paterson and Guthrie, and a close friendship grew between Hornel and George Henry.

The light, agriculture, buildings and people at Kirkcudbright were very different in comparison with those at Cockburnspath, but the Boys continued to seek inspiration from everyday life in this new setting. The town's distinctive tolbooth and eighteenth-century houses feature in their pictures. The surrounding area of Galloway provided the most enduring imagery of this period, including undulating hills, fields with cattle, woods with streams and dense undergrowth, and the changing colours of the seasons.

The sleepy village of Moniaive, in nearby Dumfriesshire, was where Paterson lived for many years. Inspired by the beauty of his local environment, he painted many landscapes of the village and the countryside around it. He used a wooden hut as a mobile studio so that, protected from the wind and rain, he could paint throughout the year in different locations.

Moniaive, 1885–6
James Paterson
Hunterian Museum and Art Gallery,
University of Glasgow

Paterson painted numerous views of the waters around Moniaive. This painting shows the Dalwhat Burn, a tributary of the Cairn Water, with the village in the distance. The gentle, muted colours and the balanced composition owe something to Whistler's harmonious 'arrangements'.

In the Town Crofts, Kirkcudbright, 1885
Edward Atkinson Hornel
Private Collection

Hornel's choice of subject and handling of landscape reveal the influence of Guthrie and Henry, and the style they had developed at Cockburnspath.

Old Willie – the Village Worthy, 1886
James Guthrie
Kelvingrove Art Gallery and Museum, Culture and Sport Glasgow

Old Willie, with his distinctive sideburns, large nose and weather-beaten cheeks, was a favourite subject for the Glasgow Boys in Kirkcudbright.

Noon, 1885
George Henry
Private Collection

Henry's debt to Bastien-Lepage is apparent in elements such as the prominent tree trunk, the solitary figure and the block-capital signature. The inclusion of the long upright stems not only adds foreground interest but also frames the girl and helps create a feeling of depth.

Symbolism

A Galloway Landscape, 1889
George Henry
Kelvingrove Art Gallery and Museum, Culture and Sport Glasgow

A typical Galloway landscape has been transformed into a flat pattern. Some critics likened this extraordinary painting to a Persian carpet.

George Henry and Edward Hornel shared ideas about art, and in time collaborated on joint works, notably *The Druids – Bringing in the Mistletoe*. This led to a major shift in their painting. Strong colours, pattern and design became increasingly important in their compositions. They used colour, brushwork and paint texture to represent – or symbolize – objects from nature that they would earlier have painted in more detail. They wanted to evoke ideas and emotion through symbolic means rather than through a literal depiction of scenes.

Horizons and perspective disappeared from their pictures, leading to an intense and claustrophobic atmosphere. They chose subjects inspired by Celtic folklore and Japanese art, rather than ones taken direct from life. These works resembled nothing else painted in Britain at the time and when exhibited in Europe received great acclaim. At the same time, some other Glasgow Boys, including David Gauld, produced equally original work.

The organizer of the annual Munich art exhibition saw paintings by the Glasgow Boys in the Grosvenor Gallery in London in 1890 and immediately asked for them for his own show in Munich later that year.

The symbolist pictures by Henry and Hornel were among those that made a huge impression with their startling new style, which outshone all the other works on display.

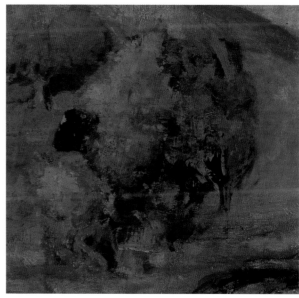

In this part of the painting, a cow seems to merge with a tree.

Saint Agnes, 1889–90
David Gauld

National Gallery of Scotland,
Edinburgh

Purchased with the aid of the Art
Fund, 1999

David Gauld was a
designer of stained glass
as well as a painter. The
bright fields, sky, river
and costume, and the
shadows, appear as flat
areas of colour, each
separated from the next
by a distinct line, as in a
stained-glass window.

The Dance of Spring,
1892–3
Edward Atkinson Hornel

Kelvingrove Art Gallery and
Museum, Culture and Sport
Glasgow

Here figures and
landscape merge
together in a riot of
colour and pattern. The
powerful suggestion of
movement and rhythm
adds to the sense of
joyous occasion.

The Druids – Bringing in the Mistletoe, 1890
George Henry and Edward Atkinson Hornel
Kelvingrove Art Gallery and Museum, Culture and
Sport Glasgow

This astonishing painting shows a group of Celtic priests or Druids in richly decorated ceremonial robes and insignia processing down a steep hillside from a sacred oak grove. Accompanying them are white wild cattle, their horns bedecked with mistletoe, a plant venerated by the Druids, who believed it had magical as well as medicinal properties. The use of gold to emphasize the importance of the principal figures was so daring that only European avant-garde artists, such as Gustav Klimt, had the courage to further develop its decorative potential.

Modern Life

Having made their reputations as painters of rural scenes, some of the Glasgow Boys – Lavery, Guthrie, Walton and Kennedy in particular – looked for new subjects in the towns. They hoped this would appeal to their existing patrons and attract new ones.

Lavery found that subjects with a middle-class flavour had a ready market. He, Guthrie and Walton gradually began to focus on well-off areas such as Helensburgh, Cathcart and parts of Paisley. Instead of rural people at work, they now began to paint people in the suburbs relaxing. They depicted sports and leisure pursuits, such as boating and cycling.

The outstanding work on this theme was Lavery's masterpiece *The Tennis Party*, which was painted at Cartbank, the Glasgow home of the artist Alexander MacBride. Hugely appreciated abroad, the work received medals in Paris and Munich.

Travel and street life also inspired the Glasgow Boys. These subjects had been favoured by the French Impressionists some years earlier, but the Boys are not known to have had any direct links with them and probably developed their interest independently.

En Plein Air or *An Afternoon Walk*, 1885
Edward Arthur Walton
Private Collection

The large areas of empty space in this careful design, together with the limited colour range, derive from Walton's admiration of Whistler. The scene is outside James Whitelaw Hamilton's home in Helensburgh.

Sundown or *River Landscape by Moonlight*, 1887
George Henry
Hunterian Museum and Art Gallery, University of Glasgow

In this atmospheric view of an industrial riverside, probably by the Clyde, at dusk, the huge globe of the sun dominates the sky. It has echoes of Whistler's nocturnes – night scenes.

Stirling Station, 1887
William Kennedy

Kelvingrove Art Gallery and Museum, Culture and Sport Glasgow

Bought with the assistance of the Heritage Lottery Fund, the Art Fund, the Hamilton Bequest and
the Friends of Glasgow Museums, 2008

Modern life is here represented by the railways, a highly unusual subject
for the Glasgow Boys. Kennedy, who favoured military themes, included
a kilted soldier from the nearby barracks at Stirling Castle.

The Tennis Party, 1885
John Lavery
Aberdeen Art Gallery & Museums Collections

The strongly horizontal format of this painting
was essential to show the whole tennis court.
Lavery has carefully balanced the figures and
evening shadows, and successfully conveyed a
sense of frozen action.

An Interruption, 1884
Alexander Roche
Private Collection

A lady relaxes out of doors, protected from the full sunlight by an umbrella. Roche's painting was possibly inspired by Lavery's modern-life subjects.

The Lure of Japan

The shapes of the lady's
hairstyle, kimono and
fan, combined with the
freedom of brushstroke,
give an almost abstract
quality to this work.
The stylized blossom
branches in the top-left
corner are loosely but
delicately painted in the
manner of Japanese
calligraphy.

Japanese art, architecture and design had a growing
influence in Europe after the country opened up to
trade with the West in 1868. French artists were the
first to respond to the art of Japan, and the fashion
spread to Britain via Whistler, who had assembled a
fine Japanese collection while living in Paris.

Japanese motifs could be seen in the Glasgow
Boys' work from the mid 1880s and it became
a major element in the paintings of Hornel and
Henry from 1888. They regarded Japan as a model
society, where people displayed a refreshing honesty,
simplicity and spirituality, completely at one with
their natural surroundings. They aimed to reflect
these qualities in their Galloway pictures.

In 1893 Henry and Hornel set out to visit Japan,
to experience at first hand the culture that had
inspired them. Their visit, which lasted 18 months,
was financed by the art dealer Alexander Reid and
the shipowner and collector William Burrell. They
were confident Henry and Hornel would return
with new works in keeping with the current taste in
Glasgow for paintings influenced by Japanese art.

Unfortunately, almost all of Henry's paintings
from Japan were ruined – they had been wrapped
for the journey before the oil paint was completely
dry. It is possible that Henry painted *Japanese Lady
with a Fan* when he returned to Glasgow, inspired by
a souvenir postcard – one of three hundred he and
Hornel brought back with them.

The two artists must have been fascinated by the
different culture they encountered. Not all elements,
however, were easy to appreciate. Musical parties
were very much part of Japanese life and often
special performances were given for foreign visitors.
Hornel said that he found the music 'maddening'.

A Music Party, 1894
Edward Atkinson Hornel

Aberdeen Art Gallery &
Museums Collections

The vertical format of
this composition is clearly
inspired by the conventions
of Japanese prints, though
Hornel's thickly applied
paint is in his own very
different style. Here we see
women playing traditional
instruments. A bonsai tree
with delicate pink blossom
and a lady serving tea
complete the scene.

The Balcony, Yokohama, 1894
Edward Atkinson Hornel
Yale Center for British Art, New Haven

Hornel often experimented with unconventional viewpoints.
Here the model's head, seen from the back, almost seems
superimposed on the background. She looks out on the junks –
traditional sailing boats – in the harbour.

New Directions in the 1890s

A Garden in France, 1898
John Lavery
Private Collection

With maturity came the confidence to paint with the delightful spontaneity that is apparent here. This work is the forerunner of the informal group portraits with which Lavery sealed his reputation.

After the formative years of the early 1880s, when their work had a clear similarity, in the 1890s the Glasgow Boys began to pursue their own individual paths. They kept their friendships, but personal reputations, new family commitments or simply a desire to break away from youthful radicalism led them in very different directions.

Some, notably the landscape painters, maintained the style of their early works. A number became successful portrait painters. Others specialized in animal or flower subjects. They were all in full control of their chosen medium, whether oil paint, watercolour or pastel. They had national reputations at home and growing international fame. No longer did they have to compete to exhibit in the major venues in Britain and Europe – now, exhibition organizers everywhere were eager to show their latest works.

The White Flower, 1897
Edward Arthur Walton
Kirkcaldy Museum & Art Gallery

There was a fashion in the 1890s for art dealers
to hold exhibitions of paintings of 'Fair Women'.
This work, with its idealized female figure, has a
dream-like romantic quality.

The Contrabandista – The Smuggler, 1892
Arthur Melville
Collection of Miss Flure Grossart

Melville saw smugglers on a hillside while travelling through
Spain. Referring to the scene, he wrote of the 'long
shadows, cold blue thrown by poplar trees' that fascinated
him. They dominate this dramatic composition.

A Lady of Fashion, 1894
George Henry
Private Collection

After Henry returned from Japan in 1894, he turned increasingly to painting fashionable ladies. He moved to London in about 1897, where he became a successful portraitist.

Artists and Studios

Left:
Hard at it, 1883
James Guthrie
Kelvingrove Art Gallery and
Museum, Culture and Sport
Glasgow

Painted on the beach
near Cockburnspath, this
picture gives us a glimpse
of Guthrie's experience of
working outside. The direct,
broad brushstrokes of the
sky show how the artist
applied his colour.

Right:
*Portrait of Joseph
Crawhall*, 1884
Edward Arthur Walton
Scottish National Portrait
Gallery, Edinburgh

Walton shows Crawhall
standing against the back
of a large canvas. An
inscription near the top-
right-hand corner says 'Joe
Crawhall / The Impressionist
/ By EA Walton / The
Realist'. Both artists were
poking fun at attempts to
categorize them.

The Glasgow Boys did not produce formal portraits
of each other, but sometimes painted slightly light-
hearted pictures of themselves at work or at leisure.
They also recorded studio life, as is best shown by
works by Lavery. His pictures of models in the studio
or the parlour, painted either in France or in Glasgow
in the 1880s, depict his working environment
in the winter months. His own paintings can be
seen carefully arranged in the background. In
reality studios were less tidy, as we can see from
photographs of the time.

In some delightful, small sketches of artists at
work, the Glasgow Boys also recorded a key element
of their summer working practice – painting out of
doors. Such works often show an umbrella, which
was used as protection from the sun and to lessen its
dazzling effect on white canvas. Portable 'studios',
which would all fit into a satchel, would also include
ingenious easels, paint tubes, containers for liquids,
brushes and small sketching panels.

A Quiet Day in the Studio, 1883
John Lavery
Kelvingrove Art Gallery and Museum,
Culture and Sport Glasgow

A model sits resting in Lavery's Paris studio, with a large canvas in the background. The pose of the model and limited colour show the influence of Whistler, who exhibited his famous portrait *Arrangement in Grey and Black: Portrait of the Painter's Mother* at the Paris Salon the same year as this work was painted.

Study for A Pupil of Mine, Grez-sur-Loing, 1883
John Lavery
Private Collection, Switzerland

Despite its title, when this study was painted Lavery was not established enough to have recognized pupils, but at the colony at Grez many informal relationships were struck up between the artists who came there.

SKETCH FOR LARGE PICTURE

J LAVERY 188

The Ropewalk, 1888
James Guthrie
Private Collection

The rope works at
Cambuskenneth provided
stunning light effects, and
Guthrie took advantage of the
brown paper he worked on to
enhance both the deep shadows
and areas of bright daylight.
The girl turns a handle to twist
together the strands of rope.

James Guthrie's Pastels

Towards the end of the 1880s there was growing interest in the medium of pastel, and the Grosvenor Gallery in London devoted exhibitions to it in 1888 and 1890. Subtle or vibrant colours, usually drawn on grey- or buff-coloured paper, gave artists opportunities for startling new effects and, unlike oil paintings, pastels could be completed quickly.

Crawhall, Melville and Walton worked occasionally in pastel, but it was Guthrie who most explored the medium. Guthrie produced his first pastels at Cambuskenneth, near Stirling. These show the village and surrounding countryside, including the local rope works.

A second series centred on life in Helensburgh, where Guthrie had stayed in the early 1880s. These depict the town and shore, nearby farms, navvies working on the railway and studies of middle-class life, similar in subject to Walton's watercolours.

The majority of Guthrie's pastels were exhibited in 1890–91, first at Dowdeswell's in London, where nothing sold, and then at Lawrie's in Glasgow, where every work sold.

The Morning Paper, 1890
James Guthrie
Private Collection

The organizers of major public exhibitions expected all drawings and watercolours to be displayed in gold frames. When Guthrie showed his pastels at Dowdeswell's in London, he cheekily framed them in silver.

Tennis, 1890
James Guthrie
Private Collection

Tennis was a fashionable
sport in the west of
Scotland, as shown
previously by Lavery's
painting *The Tennis
Party*. Guthrie made a
few pastels showing
Helensburgh girls either
watching or playing.

Firelight Reflections, 1890
James Guthrie

Paisley Art Institute Collection, held by
Paisley Museum, Renfrewshire Council

Guthrie has used pastel to show the glow of the fire and the roaring
flames. This room is thought to be in the house of Mrs Whyte, widow of
Dr Whyte who had allowed Guthrie the use of his studio to paint early
pictures such as *To Pastures New*.

52

John Lavery at the Glasgow International Exhibition, 1888

The Glasgow International Exhibition, 1888
John Lavery
Kelvingrove Art Gallery and Museum, Culture and Sport Glasgow

In this painting, which may have been originally entitled *Fairy Lights*, we see the crowd thronging across the bridge over the River Kelvin under a crescent moon. The Japanese lanterns, as well as the restrained colour harmonies, make this one of the most Whistlerian of the series.

The Glasgow International Exhibition of 1888 provided Lavery with an excellent opportunity to paint a series of fifty small lively oils. These were then exhibited to considerable acclaim at the Craibe Angus Gallery in Glasgow. They showed many different facets of the exhibition, which transformed Kelvingrove Park. The specially erected exhibition buildings, though only temporary, were so elaborate that some people likened the exhibition area to Baghdad. Restaurants included the Bishop's Castle Tearoom, with waitresses dressed as Mary, Queen of Scots, and the Indian Restaurant, which served what were at the time very exotic dishes.

Lavery painted the tea rooms, the exhibition stands and the crowds watching military displays. He made studies of shop assistants and chefs, of ladies promenading, and even of a gondola on the River Kelvin. Whistler was his inspiration, particularly in the handling of twilight and night effects.

There was no catalogue for Lavery's exhibition, and so many of the paintings are now known by descriptive titles, which may not have been the ones Lavery used himself.

On a more formal level, Lavery was awarded the commission to paint a record of the state visit of Queen Victoria to the exhibition, a huge group portrait of more than 250 people, which laid the grounds for much of his future success.

People from all walks of life attended the 1888 exhibition.

Left:
The Blue Hungarians at the Glasgow International Exhibition, 1888
John Lavery
Fleming Collection, London

There were entertainments offered daily throughout the exhibition, including a varied programme at the bandstand. William Johnson's Blue Gypsy String Band played under the conductor Herr Barzea for three weeks from 4 June, and were paid £375.

Right:
A View from the Canal at the Glasgow International Exhibition, 1888
John Lavery
Cecil Higgins Art Gallery, Bedford

The River Kelvin is the subject of this painting, despite its misleading title which was given on account of the still nature of the water and the presence of the Venetian gondola.

The Dutch Cocoa House, 1888
John Lavery
National Gallery of Scotland, Edinburgh
Purchased with the aid of the Barrogill Keith Bequest Fund, 1985

The Dutch chocolate company Van Houten built a Cocoa House at the 1888 Glasgow International Exhibition. It was in 16th-century Dutch style and decorated with blue-and-white tiles. The attractive interior was the setting for one of Lavery's most successful pictures in his series.

58

Arthur Melville's Watercolours

Brig o'Turk, 1893
Arthur Melville
Robertson Collection, Orkney

Melville was at Brig o'Turk in the Trossachs in 1893, ten years after the Glasgow Boys first discovered the village. The fiery autumn colours gave him the opportunity to create this stunning watercolour.

Melville was one of the finest watercolour painters of all time. He could work with an earthy palette, in the rustic realist manner of the Glasgow Boys, or with strong colour and saturated light as in his Spanish, North African and Middle Eastern subjects. He seems to have been attracted to watercolour because of his natural talents – there appears to have been no teacher or influence that shaped his style. He usually laid his background on damp paper, and when this was nearly dry he added his typical bright patches of colour.

Experiences overseas inspired many of Melville's watercolours and his most striking compositions followed a great adventure that he began in 1880, spending the next two years journeying to Egypt, the Arabian Peninsula, Iraq and as far as India. The intense heat and light and the exotic surroundings, not to mention being attacked and left for dead by robbers, had a profound effect on his artistic output. He continually returned to sketches and memories from these travels. The six visits Melville made to Spain between 1890 and 1899 inspired some of his most glorious works.

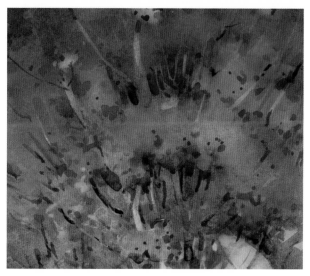

As here, Melville sometimes used the technique known as 'blottesque' – meaning 'like blots of paint'. He applied drops of watercolour paint with a heavily loaded brush, flooding areas of paper so that the colours mixed together on the surface, creating brilliant effects.

Awaiting an Audience with the Pasha, 1887
Arthur Melville
Private Collection

This is the most dramatic of Melville's Orientalist pictures and was praised for being 'in the best contemporary French manner'. The tension mounts in the Ottoman palace as the petitioners await their fate.

Seated Peasant Girl, 1878
Arthur Melville
Private Collection

This very early work was painted in France in 1878. Melville's watercolours so impressed Crawhall, Henry and Walton that they soon began to use the medium themselves.

The Sapphire Sea, Passages,
1892
Arthur Melville
Scottish Gallery, Edinburgh

In contrast to the translucency of
conventional watercolour, in this
work Melville has used several
coats of ultramarine to create
a stunning velvety depth to the
sea. This is a perfect foil for the
dazzling white of the walls and
busy figures, some achieved by the
skilful use of blank paper, some
by the application of the thick
pigment known as 'Chinese white'.

62

Joseph Crawhall's Watercolours

The Aviary, Clifton, 1888
Joseph Crawhall
The Burrell Collection, Culture and Sport Glasgow

This watercolour painting earned a gold medal at the groundbreaking Munich exhibition of 1890, where the Glasgow Boys' reputation in Europe was secured.

Crawhall began painting in watercolour early in his career. Melville seems to have influenced his first works, in which we see intense, almost blinding light, and deep, dark shadows.

The Aviary, Clifton established Crawhall's reputation, giving him the confidence to develop a deeply personal technique. As we can see in *The White Drake*, he often worked on holland, a buff-coloured linen, and used gouache, an opaque water-based paint. Crawhall created perfect gouaches from memory, without using preliminary sketches, following careful observation of his subject, often an animal or bird.

Crawhall was a huntsman, rider, amateur jockey and horse breeder; indeed, his love of horses was as great as his love of painting.

The unusual viewpoint in *The Aviary, Clifton* makes for a huge difference in scale. The foreground parrots dominate the two fashionably dressed ladies, who are almost unnoticeable at first glance. The composition suggests the influence of Japanese art.

A Black Rabbit, about 1894
Joseph Crawhall
Yale Center for British Art, New Haven

This apparently simple composition consists of several layers of semi-transparent washes to create a faultless image. If Crawhall was at all dissatisfied with something he was working on, he would destroy the picture.

The Byre, 1887
Joseph Crawhall
Kelvingrove Art Gallery and Museum, Culture and Sport Glasgow

Crawhall transfers the sunlight of his pictures of Tangier, Morocco, to a Scottish scene. This painting of a boy watching over a bull was originally titled *Left in Charge*.

Horse and Cart with Lady,
about 1894–1900
Joseph Crawhall

Kelvingrove Art Gallery and
Museum, Culture and Sport
Glasgow

This composition, with half
of the cart and lady cut off
at the left, and a daringly flat
pattern formed by the kerbed
flowerbeds, recalls Whistler,
Japanese prints and even
Degas.

The White Drake, about 1895
Joseph Crawhall
National Gallery of Scotland, Edinburgh

Purchased with support from the National Lottery through
the Heritage Lottery Fund and the Art Fund, 1996

This gouache is usually held to be Crawhall's masterpiece. It epitomizes his classic technique:
he built up the white areas layer by layer – a reversal of the approach in a standard
watercolour – while one or two applications sufficed for the darker background areas.

Into the Twentieth Century

By 1900 few of the Boys remained in Glasgow – London, and sometimes Edinburgh, became favoured bases, if often only temporary ones. But they maintained their presence in the annual exhibitions in Glasgow, some until the 1940s. Only Melville, whose work continued to challenge convention and extend the Boys' radical reputations, died young, in 1904 of typhoid fever caught in Spain.

Their styles further diverged, with an emphasis on portraiture. Lavery and Guthrie ranked among the leading portraitists of their day. Lavery's fascination with London and Irish society led him to become a painter of royalty and, later, of Hollywood film stars. Others followed quieter lives, respected and admired, but no longer pioneering new movements in art.

By 1900 the Glasgow Boys had achieved their aims and more. Many had become members of the Royal Scottish Academy or the Royal Academy, though Hornel refused to comply and declined his invitation. Guthrie even became President of the Royal Scottish Academy in 1902, followed by Paterson in 1922. Some became rich, some acquired international clients and reputations, most saw their work enter museums across the world. They were a force to be reckoned with. They had arrived.

But at heart, as Robert Macaulay Stevenson, later historian of the group, said in 1941, 'We were just the Boys'.